A Place to Call Home

by Ellen Lawrence

Published in 2015 by Ruby Tuesday Books Ltd.

Editor: Mark J. Sachner
Designer: Emma Randall
Production: John Lingham

Photo credits:
Alamy: 4 (right), 5 (top), 6 (top), 7, 8 (top), 12 (top), 16–17, 19 (top), 22; Corbis: 14, 20–21, 22; FLPA: 4 (left), 6 (bottom); Istockphoto: 9, 18–19, 22; Major Multimedia/Lauren Major: Cover; Shutterstock: 5 (bottom), 8 (bottom), 10–11, 12 (left), 12 (right), 13, 15, 18 (bottom), 22, 23; Superstock: 4 (center).

Library of Congress Control Number: 2014958140

ISBN 978-1-910549-02-5

Printed and published in the United States of America

For further information including rights and permissions requests, please contact our Customer Service Department at 877-337-8577.

The picture on the front cover of this book shows a houseboat on Tonlé Sap lake in Cambodia. Turn to page 8 to find out more about the people who live on the lake.

Contents

Words shown in **bold** in the text are explained in the glossary.

All the places in this book are shown on the map on page 22.

What Is a Home?

A home is a place to stay cool.

A home is a place to stay dry.

A home is a place to stay warm.

4

A home is a place
to be with the
people you love.

A home is a place
to feel safe.

Everybody needs
a place to
call home.

5

A Himba Hut

The Himba people of Namibia live in small villages. Sometimes they move from place to place to find grass for their goats and cattle.

Wherever they settle, Himba people build small homes called **huts**.

Milking the goats

A Himba hut

The huts are made of branches covered with dried mud and cow dung.

When Himba children are very young, they live and sleep in a hut with their parents. Once they are about three years old, they leave their parents' hut. Then they share a hut with other children.

A Floating Village

On a huge lake in Cambodia, people live in floating villages.

The children who live here travel to their schools by boat.

At lunchtime they buy food from a floating food cart.

A floating school

A floating food cart

A floating church

Some families make their homes in houses that float on the water. Others live on houseboats.

The lake is called Tonlé Sap (TUHN-lay SAHP). Some of the homes on the lake have floating gardens. There are floating shops, gas stations, churches, and even floating basketball courts!

A house and garden

9

Rainbow Homes in the Snow

On the tiny island of Kulusuk, the land turns white in winter.
There's still a rainbow of colors to be seen, however.

That's because everyone on Kulusuk lives in
brightly painted wooden houses.

Kulusuk is just off the coast of Greenland.

The island is home to fewer than 300 people.

Lots of sled dogs live on Kulusuk. They pull the sleds that people use to travel over the ice and snow.

Almost no trees grow in Greenland, so there's no wood for construction. People on Kulusuk build their wooden houses from kits. All the pieces of a house are sent by boat from Denmark. Then the owners fit the pieces together to make their new home.

Living in a City

Around the world, billions of people live in big cities.

A city can be a noisy place with lots of traffic jams.

Many city homes do not have a garden or yard. People spend time outdoors in parks and playgrounds.

A crowded street in Kathmandu in Nepal

San Francisco in the United States

Some people in a city live in houses.

Apartment blocks in Hong Kong

Many people in cities live in apartments high above the ground.

A Home in a City Slum

Not everybody who lives in a city has a house or apartment. Around the world, millions of very poor people make their homes in parts of cities known as **slums**.

Boys in Delhi keep warm around a fire made of garbage.

In the city of Delhi in India, thousands of people live in slums.

They build small homes from materials they find on the streets and on garbage dumps.

The homes have no electricity, toilets, or water for drinking, cooking, and washing.

In Delhi, thousands of families may share just one water tap in a slum area. Each day, adults and children stand in line for hours to fill buckets and plastic bottles with water from the tap. Sometimes, however, the water is not clean. Then people get sick when they drink it.

A House with a Tower

On the Indonesian island of Sumba, people live in small villages. Each village is made up of houses that have towers on the roofs.

In a Sumba village there are many large stone **monuments**.

These are the tombstones of villagers who have died throughout the centuries.

A tombstone

A water buffalo

The people of Sumba are farmers.

They raise pigs, water buffaloes, and chickens.

The tower of a Sumba house is used as a safe place to keep precious objects. People believe that the **spirits** of their **ancestors** live in the towers of their homes.

The roof of a Sumba house is thatched with grasses.

Animals live in the bottom part of the house.

People live in this part of the house.

17

A Home on the Move

Many people in Mongolia raise horses, cattle, camels, sheep, and goats. They are **nomads** who move from place to place to find fresh grass for their animals.

When you're on the move, you need a home that can move, too.

Mongolian nomads live in tent-like homes called *gers*.

A camel carrying a ger

People in Mongolia have lived in gers for at least 3,000 years. A ger has a wooden frame. The frame is covered with layers of felt made from sheep's wool. It has an outer covering made from waterproof canvas.

Children watching TV inside their family's ger

It takes less than an hour to build or dismantle a ger!

A Place to Call Home

Every year, many people around the world have to leave their homes. Sometimes this happens because of a natural disaster such as a flood or earthquake. Sometimes it's because of war.

In 2011 a war began in Syria.

Millions of people left their homes to escape from danger.

They became **refugees** and had to find safety in camps in Syria and in neighboring countries.

People who become refugees don't only leave their homes. They leave behind family, friends, and pets. Children have to leave behind their toys. There may be nowhere for children to go to school.

Many refugees live in a camp for years.

They hope that one day it will be safe to go home.

Children from Syria at a refugee camp

Where in the World?

Canada
Page 4

Kulusuk, Greenland
Pages 10–11

England
Page 12

Syria
Pages 20–21

Nepal
Page 12

Mongolia
Pages 18–19

United States
Page 12

North America

Europe

Asia

China
Page 5

United States
Page 5

Africa

South America

Australia

Hong Kong, China
Page 13

India
Pages 14–15

Brazil
Page 4

Senegal
Page 4

Namibia
Pages 6–7

Kenya
Page 5

Cambodia
Pages 8–9

Sumba, Indonesia
Pages 16–17

Glossary

ancestor (AN-sess-tur)
A relative who lived a long time ago. For example, your great-grandparents and great-great-grandparents are your ancestors.

hut (HUT)
A small house that usually has just one room and one story.

kit (KIT)
A collection of objects, such as pieces of wood, that can be fitted together to make something, for example, a piece of furniture or a complete house.

monument (MON-yoo-muhnt)
A statue or other structure that is usually made of stone. A monument is made as a way to remember someone who has died and it is often placed on a person's grave.

nomad (NOH-mad)
A person who regularly moves from one area to another and does not live in one place all the time.

refugee (REF-yoo-jee)
A person who has been forced to leave his or her home to escape danger and needs to be protected.

slum (SLUHM)
An overcrowded and often dirty area where many people live in poverty. A slum is usually in a city or on the edge of a city.

spirit (SPIHR-it)
An invisible part of a person that many people believe lives on after death. For example, a ghost is a type of spirit.

Index

Read More

Lewis, Clare. *Homes Around the World (Acorn)*. North Mankato, MN: Heinemann-Raintree (2015).

Morris, Ann. *Houses and Homes (Around the World)*. New York: Harper Collins (1992).

Learn More Online

To learn more about homes around the world, go to
www.rubytuesdaybooks.com/homes